CELEBRATING THE CITY OF QUITO

Celebrating the City of Quito

Walter the Educator

Silent King Books
A WhichHead Entertainment Imprint

Copyright © 2024 by Walter the Educator

All rights reserved. No part of this book may be reproduced in any manner whatsoever without written per- mission except in the case of brief quotations embodied in critical articles and reviews.

First Printing, 2024

Disclaimer

This book is a literary work; the story is not about specific persons, locations, situations, and/or circumstances unless mentioned in a historical context. Any resemblance to real persons, locations, situations, and/or circumstances is coincidental. This book is for entertainment and informational purposes only. The author and publisher offer this information without warranties expressed or implied. No matter the grounds, neither the author nor the publisher will be accountable for any losses, injuries, or other damages caused by the reader's use of this book. The use of this book acknowledges an understanding and acceptance of this disclaimer.

Celebrating the City of Quito is a little collectible souvenir book that belongs to the Celebrating Cities Book Series by Walter the Educator. Collect them all and more books at WaltertheEducator.com

USE THE EXTRA SPACE TO TAKE NOTES AND DOCUMENT YOUR MEMORIES

QUITO

In the heart of Andean peaks where legends softly lie,

Celebrating the City of
Quito

Quito's essence rises, a jewel set against the sky.

Beneath the equatorial sun, its soul breathes ancient lore,

Where past and present meld as one on pathways cobblestoned.

Cradle of the Condor's flight, where history finds its voice,

Whispers of Inca empire's might and Spanish conquerors' choice.

A city kissed by Time's own hand, where churches pierce the blue,

Carving tales in stone and sand, each shadow, dusk, and hue.

From Pichincha's mighty slope, where clouds in silence cling,

To valleys where the secrets of lost epochs gently sing,

Quito's streets, alive with dreams, pulse with a fervent beat,

In markets, plazas, ancient beams, the old and new worlds meet.

La Ronda's lanes, a festive cheer, with artisans at play,

Where melodies and laughter hear the end of day's array.

Balconies adorned with flowers, a palette bright and fair,

In evening's calm and twilight hours, romance perfumes the air.

Celebrating the City of
Quito

Gothic spires of La Basílica rise, a testament of grace,

Their shadows dance, where old faith ties to new hope's eager face.

The Virgin of El Panecillo, arms spread wide and vast,

A guardian of the city, still, a bridge from future to the past.

Carmen Alto's solemn hush, cloisters steeped in prayer,

Echoes of devotion rush, through hallowed, sacred air.

San Francisco's plaza broad, a mingling of delight,

Where travelers trod and natives nod, beneath the Andes' sight.

In Mariscal's vibrant pulse, where night ignites the streets,

The young, the old, all cultures merge in rhythm's diverse beats.

Gastronomy's rich symphony, in flavors bold and rare,

From ceviche's briny glee to llapingachos' flair.

TeléfériQo's ascent, where vistas grandly sprawl,

An elevation of content, where city's essence calls.

Above the clouds, perspectives shift, horizons vast and free,

Celebrating the City of
Quito

Quito's spirit, pure and swift, in every breath we see.

Museums tell their guarded tales, of gold and ancient clay,

Of how the past in Quito sails, into tomorrow's day.

Casa del Alabado's trove, where artifacts reside,

In timeless beauty they enrobe, a heritage with pride.

La Mitad del Mundo stands, a line that marks the earth,

A hemispheric clasp of hands, a symbol of rebirth.

Where north meets south, and east greets west,

In Quito's heart, we're truly blessed, with unity's attest.

Celebrating the City of
Quito

ABOUT THE CREATOR

Walter the Educator is one of the pseudonyms for Walter Anderson. Formally educated in Chemistry, Business, and Education, he is an educator, an author, a diverse entrepreneur, and he is the son of a disabled war veteran. "Walter the Educator" shares his time between educating and creating. He holds interests and owns several creative projects that entertain, enlighten, enhance, and educate, hoping to inspire and motivate you. Follow, find new works, and stay up to date with Walter the Educator™

at WaltertheEducator.com

www.ingramcontent.com/pod-product-compliance
Lightning Source LLC
LaVergne TN
LVHW012050070526
838201LV00082B/3902